Contents

Sharks

Whales

Dolphins and Porpoises

SHARKS
and other Deep Sea Creatures

Sally Morgan

Camilla de la Bédoyère

Sandy Creek

Project Editor: Carey Scott
Designers: Stefan Morris Design and Fiona Hajée
Picture Researcher: Veneta Bullen

Copyright © QED Publishing, 2010
First published in the UK in 2010

This 2010 edition published by Sandy Creek by arrangement with QEB Publishing, Inc.

Sandy Creek
122 Fifth Avenue
New York, NY 10011

ISBN 978 1 4351 2709 8

A CIP record for this book is available from the Library of Congress.

Lot 10 9 8 7 6 5 4 3 2 1

Manufactured 08/2010

Printed in China

The words in **bold** are explained in the Glossary on page 118.

Sharks

Sharks are some of the most fascinating creatures in the world, with a reputation for being deadly. They can grow bigger than a city bus, smell their prey from far away, and they have thick, rough skin that protects them—like a suit of armor!

The Shark

Sharks are the most awesome creatures in the oceans. Although they are a type of fish, they are also vertebrates, which means that they have a backbone.

On their back sharks have a large, triangular fin that sticks up out of the water when they swim near the surface. They have two large **pectoral fins,** one on each side of their body, behind their **gill slits.** They have other fins, too.

The blue shark's long pectoral fins help it swim fast.

Fact!

The biggest-ever great white was 23 ft (7 m) long and weighed about 1,450 lbs (658 kilos)!

Sharks use their **gills** to breathe in water. When they breathe, water enters their mouth. The water flows between their gills and out through the gill slits on the sides of their head.

Sharks have very wide jaws and some types, like this great white, have jagged, pointed teeth.

Flat-bodied sharks hunt on the seabed.

Shark Types

With more than 360 different species, divided into 30 separate families, sharks range incredibly in size, from as small as a person's hand to bigger than a bus.

More than half of all sharks are less than 3 feet (about 1 meter) long. The largest sharks, such as the whale shark and the hammerhead shark, live far out in the open oceans.

The enormous basking shark often swims at the water's surface to feed.

Tiger sharks can be up to 20 ft (6 m) long.

Rare and common sharks

Some types of shark are becoming more rare, such as the basking shark. The dogfish shark and the bull shark are far more common.

Fact!

The biggest shark is the whale shark, which grows up to 50 ft (15 m) long. The smallest types grow to just 7 in (18 cm) long.

Where Do Sharks Live?

Sharks live in all the oceans of the world, apart from the coldest waters of the Antarctic.

Some sharks stay in the same region for their whole lives, and others swim from ocean to ocean. Many sharks always live in the open ocean, thousands of miles from land. Others stay in shallow waters close to the beach.

The sixgill shark is a deepwater shark.

Areas where sharks are found.

North America

Europe

Asia

Atlantic Ocean

Africa

Pacific Ocean

South America

Pacific Ocean

Indian Ocean

Australia

Southern Ocean

Antarctica

Ocean habitats

Some sharks stay close to the ocean floor, for example wobbegongs and angel sharks. Others stay hidden in the deep waters.

The sandbar shark is often found in sandy shallow waters.

Greenland Shark

Greenland sharks live in the freezing waters of the Arctic. Like many other animals that live in cold places, these giant sharks move slowly and live long lives—to the age of 100 or more.

Eating habits

Greenland sharks eat almost any creatures, from small squid to whales and seals, and even dead animals. They have about 100 little teeth, which they use to seize their **prey**.

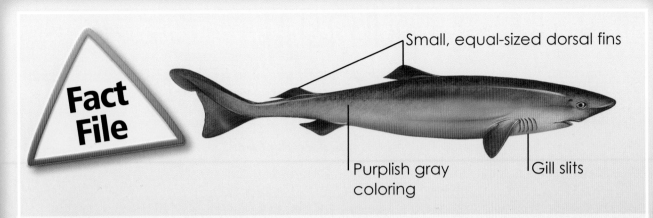

Fact File

Small, equal-sized dorsal fins

Purplish gray coloring

Gill slits

LENGTH	18 feet (5.5 meters)
HABITAT	Deep, cold ocean. Sometimes in bays and estuaries
DEPTH	Down to more than one mile (1,609 meters)
RANGE	North Atlantic Ocean and up to the Arctic region

Although these sharks usually swim slowly, they can move with great bursts of speed when they are hunting.

Giving Birth

Most types of shark give birth to their pups. The mothers keep their growing young inside their bodies to protect them from predators.

After mating, the female shark keeps the eggs inside her body. This gives them a good chance of surviving until adulthood. The growing pups get food from the egg yolk, or directly from the mother's body.

Fact!

Some shark pups eat each other while still inside their mother's body, until just one survives!

Hammerhead sharks gather together in shoals at breeding time.

Most shark pups are born tail first, like this lemon shark pup. A remora fish is watching the birth.

Nurseries

Mother sharks usually give birth in shallow waters, such as coasts and bays. These birthing places are called nurseries. There is plenty of food for the pups to eat there, such as small fish, shellfish, and worms.

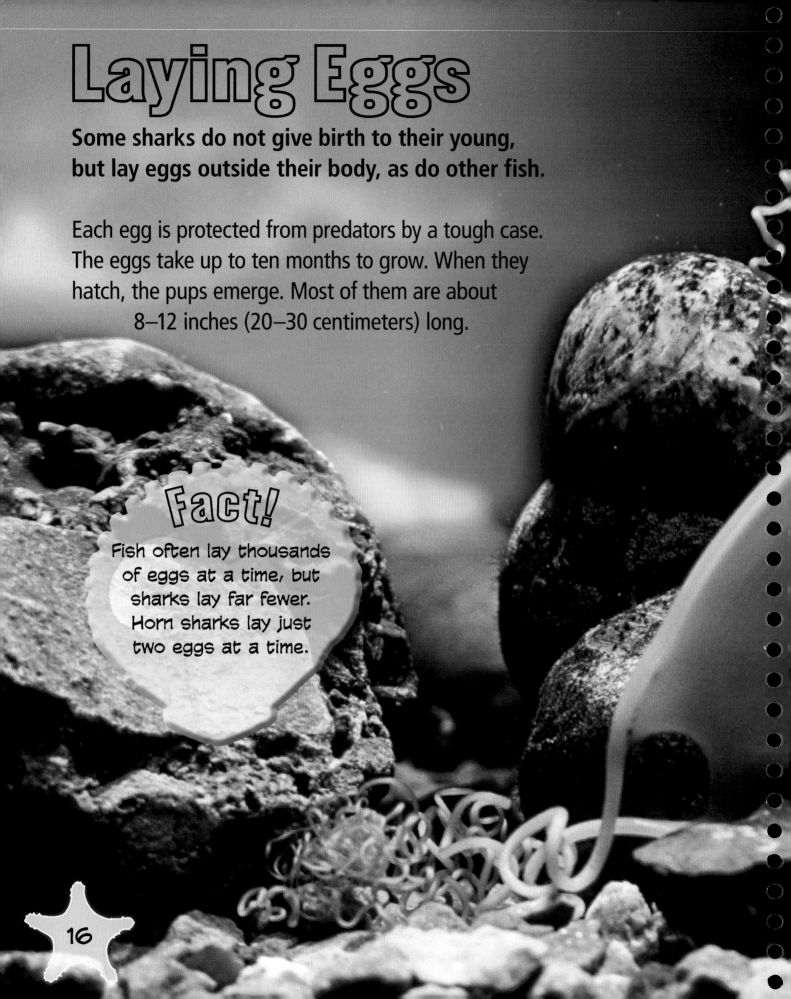

Laying Eggs

Some sharks do not give birth to their young, but lay eggs outside their body, as do other fish.

Each egg is protected from predators by a tough case. The eggs take up to ten months to grow. When they hatch, the pups emerge. Most of them are about 8–12 inches (20–30 centimeters) long.

Fact!

Fish often lay thousands of eggs at a time, but sharks lay far fewer. Horn sharks lay just two eggs at a time.

Shark pups

Baby sharks are called pups, and look like miniature adult sharks. They even have a full set of teeth. As soon as they hatch out, they can take care of themselves.

Cat shark pup

The dogfish shark's egg case anchors itself to rocks or seaweed to stop it floating away.

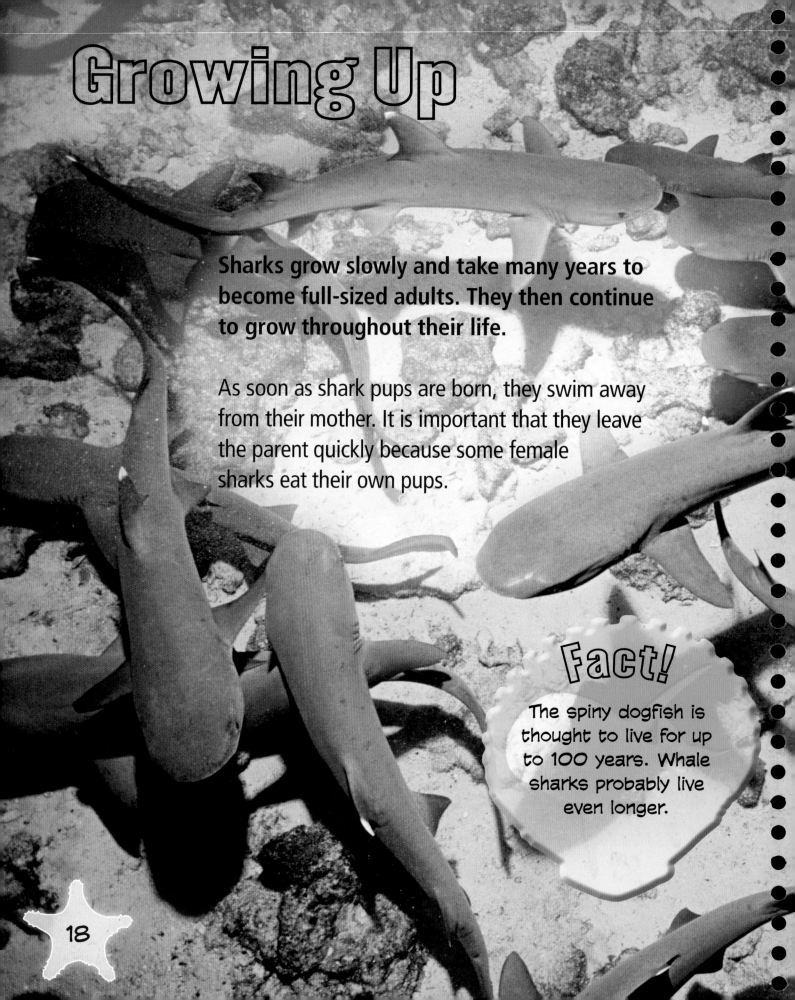

Growing Up

Sharks grow slowly and take many years to become full-sized adults. They then continue to grow throughout their life.

As soon as shark pups are born, they swim away from their mother. It is important that they leave the parent quickly because some female sharks eat their own pups.

Fact!

The spiny dogfish is thought to live for up to 100 years. Whale sharks probably live even longer.

18

This great white shark has a lot of scars and may be very old.

How long do sharks live?

Nobody is sure how long sharks live. Most of them probably live for less than 25 years, but a few types of shark have been known to live for much longer. Some of the larger species of female shark are not ready to breed until the female is between six and 18 years old. Most females produce young every two years.

Sharks gradually grow larger as they get older.

Frilled Shark

Frilled sharks are more similar to types of sharks that existed 350 million years ago than to any living sharks. They are rare animals that live in very deep water, so humans hardly ever see them.

Frilled sharks are named for their 12 frilly gill slits—six on each side of the head.

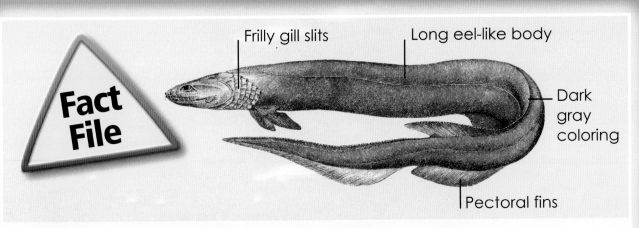

Fact File

Frilly gill slits

Long eel-like body

Dark gray coloring

Pectoral fins

LENGTH Up to 6 ¼ feet (almost 2 meters)
HABITAT Deep water, shores, and occasionally at the surface
DEPTH 330–4,000 feet (100–1,200 meters)
RANGE Scattered areas around the world, in cool and warm waters

Lifestyle

Female frilled sharks give birth to around ten pups at a time, and each one is about 20 inches (50 centimeters) long. Scientists think that these unusual sharks live for 50 years or more.

21

Swimming

A shark must keep swimming or it will sink. It has to swerve to avoid hitting something, as it cannot stop moving.

Some species, such as the great white shark, push themselves through the water using the force of their powerful tail. Other sharks, for example the whale shark, thrust their bodies from side to side to propel themselves through the water. Their large fins help them balance.

Changing direction

Sharks cannot swim backward because their large pectoral fins are not able to bend upward like other fish. If a shark needs to move backward, it allows itself to be carried back by the water or swims back around in a circle.

At night, Port Jackson sharks stop swimming and sink to the seabed.

A horn shark resting on the seabed.

Large pectoral fins behind the gill slits help with balance.

Color and Patterns

Many sharks are dull colors, such as brown, gray, or black. These colors help them stay hidden in the deep, dark water.

Zebra shark pups have stripes or spots, which are a type of **camouflage**. Camouflage helps them hide among seaweeds and in shallow water. As they grow they swim out to the deep ocean, and some of their stripy markings fade away.

When prey swims past, the wobbegong opens its large mouth. It sucks in water, pulling the prey into its mouth.

Invisible fish

A wobbegong shark's flat body, pattern of blotches, and frilled skin make it hard to spot on the seabed. Fish and squid that swim above mistake the shark for coral, rocks, or seaweed.

Many sharks have a white belly. This helps them to become invisible when seen from below against the light sky.

Fact!

Shark skin is made of tiny plates, called denticles, which are very similar in structure to teeth!

On the Move

Some sharks spend most of their lives in one area. Others, however, travel long distances in search of food, or to breed.

These journeys are called **migrations**. Female blue sharks are known to travel an incredible 4,250 miles (6,840 kilometers) in a single migration.

Fact!

Some deepwater sharks make vertical journeys every day—swimming up to the surface at night to feed.

Thresher sharks use their large tail to hit and stun their prey. They sometimes hunt in groups.

Seasonal homes

In the spring, thresher sharks move north to the cool waters of the northern Atlantic Ocean. Here they find lots of food, such as mackerel. At the end of the summer, they swim south to the warmer waters of the tropics, where they stay throughout the winter.

The blue shark has a thin snout and long pectoral fins.

Shortfin Mako Shark

The shortfin mako is the fastest of all sharks, speeding through the ocean at around 42 miles (70 kilometers) per hour. Their slender, long bodies, and small, bullet-shaped heads are streamlined—which means they are designed for slicing through water.

Big leaps

Shortfin makos are not only fast swimmers, they can also jump out of the water—leaping more than 20 feet (6 meters) into the air to avoid predators.

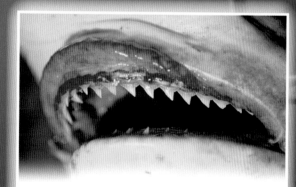

Rows of long, thin teeth are ideal for grabbing hold of slippery fish and squid.

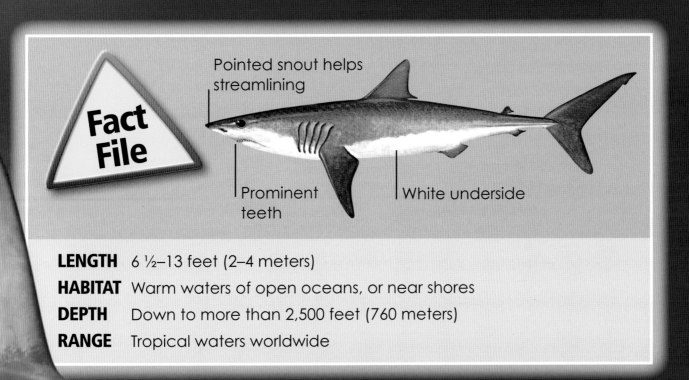

Fact File

Pointed snout helps streamlining

Prominent teeth

White underside

LENGTH	6 ½–13 feet (2–4 meters)
HABITAT	Warm waters of open oceans, or near shores
DEPTH	Down to more than 2,500 feet (760 meters)
RANGE	Tropical waters worldwide

These powerful fish are packed with muscles. They can move in bursts of very high speed to pursue their prey.

29

Shark Teeth

A shark's teeth can be big or small, sharp or blunt, jagged or smooth. Sharks have teeth that are the right size and shape for the type of food they eat.

Flat teeth are suitable for crunching snails, crabs, and sea urchins, whereas jagged teeth are ideal for chewing larger animals. Sharks can open their mouth extremely wide to swallow large prey.

As sharks get older, their teeth get larger. So the oldest sharks have the largest teeth.

30

Replacing teeth

Shark pups are born with a full set of teeth already in place. They are the same as adult teeth, but smaller. All sharks have several rows of teeth, but most use only their front row when feeding. The other rows are replacement teeth, to use when the original teeth wear away or fall out.

Every time a shark catches prey, it loses a few teeth. These are quickly replaced by new ones.

What Do Sharks Eat?

Sharks are predators. This means that they hunt and eat other animals in order to survive.

Although sharks eat a variety of foods, their diet is made up of mainly fish and **invertebrates**, such as squid and octopuses. Larger sharks catch bigger prey, including turtles, seals, and even dolphins. Some sharks eat animals that live on the seabed, such as crabs, starfish, sea urchins, and sea anemones.

This large shark is surrounded by smaller fish. Fish is a favorite food of most sharks.

32

Feeding frenzy

When sharks find their prey they sometimes go into a feeding frenzy. This behavior happens when they find a group of injured or trapped fish, or another large source of food near the shore. The sharks become very excited and thrash around in the water, before moving in for the kill.

A horn shark gobbles up squid eggs.

Fact!

Some deep-sea sharks have chemicals in their skin, which they use to make light in order to attract prey.

Hunting

Sharks hunt in different ways and many attack their prey from below. A hungry shark lurks in the deep water and charges upward out of the darkness when it spots its prey.

When hunting, the thresher shark takes full advantage of its long, sturdy tail. Once it spots a school of fish, it uses its mighty tail to herd the fish together. Then, the thresher shark uses it to stun its prey with powerful slaps.

Some sharks lie in wait for their prey.

Hunting groups

Although most sharks hunt alone, a few species hunt in groups callled shivers. Shivers of sand tiger sharks, for example, herd schools of fish into shallow water, where they can attack them more easily. Shark pups have to learn to hunt alone, and many die before they are fully grown.

Hunting in groups helps sharks catch prey.

Great White Shark

Great white sharks are probably the most feared sharks of all. They are large, powerful predators that come close to shores where people play and work. But, although they have been known to eat humans, they much prefer fish, seals, rays, dolphins, and sea turtles.

Warm bodies

Great whites can keep their body warmer than the surrounding water, so that they can remain active, alert, and fast when other fish are slowed down by the cold water.

These mighty beasts sometimes leap right out of the water.

Fact File

Triangular dorsal fin

Conical snout

Flat, triangular shaped teeth

Light underside

LENGTH	Up to 20 feet (6 meters)
HABITAT	Prefers water near the surface, and swims close to shores
DEPTH	Usually down to 820 feet (250 meters)
RANGE	Widespread through most oceans

37

Scavengers

A scavenger is an animal that eats dead animals or plants, or other food that might be considered garbage. Many types of sharks are scavengers.

Although most sharks are predators that hunt and kill fresh prey, many will also scavenge for food. Hunting is dangerous and tiring, and scavenging food can be an easier and safer way to eat.

Tiger sharks get their name from faint stripes on their sides or dorsal fin.

Fact!

Tiger sharks have been found with car tires and licence number plates in their stomach.

Unfussy eaters

Tiger sharks are well-known scavengers. Although they hunt their prey, they will also eat things that are not food at all! But, if something it has eaten gives the shark a stomachache, it turns its stomach inside out and pushes the troubling thing out of its mouth.

The gray nurse shark has been known to eat up its own pups.

Plankton Eaters

The whale shark is not only the largest shark, it is also the world's biggest fish.

Both the whale shark and the giant basking shark are **filter feeders**. They eat **plankton**—tiny plants and animals that float in the water.

This whale shark has unwelcome visitors—remora fish—attached to its body.

Scoop and suck

Filter-feeding sharks feed by swimming steadily forward with their huge mouth wide open, scooping up water and plankton as they go. The seawater flows through their gills, where it is filtered. Then the shark eats the food that is trapped.

The whale shark's enormous gill slits stretch almost all the way around its head.

40

A whale shark is about 45 ft (14 m) long and makes the diver swimming nearby look tiny.

Fact!

About 240,000 gallons (908,000 liters) of water pass through the enormous gills of the basking shark every hour when it is feeding.

Megamouth Shark

Megamouths are probably the most mysterious sharks—fewer than 50 of them have ever been spotted by humans! They probably spend most of the day deep under water, and swim to the surface at night to feed. These sharks do not need speed to hunt their prey, so their body is broad and flabby.

Filter feeders

Along with whale sharks and basking sharks, megamouths eat by filter-feeding. They swim with their enormous mouth wide open and sift plankton—tiny animals and plants—from the water.

The megamouth's massive mouth is lined with up to 50 rows of small teeth. It uses only the front three rows.

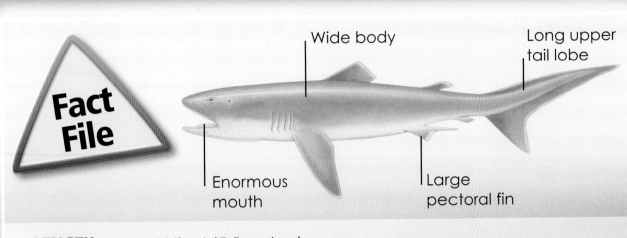

Fact File

Wide body

Long upper tail lobe

Enormous mouth

Large pectoral fin

LENGTH	Up to 18 feet (5.5 meters)
HABITAT	Prefers open water, but sometimes moves inshore
DEPTH	Mostly below 660 feet (200 meters)
RANGE	Warm, tropical waters

Shark Senses

Sharks use their senses to get information about what is going on around them. Sight is useful in the ocean's upper layers, where light can still reach.

Deep down, little light passes through the murky water. Sharks that live in deeper water have large eyes to help them detect the light.

Some sharks that live on the seafloor have hanging tendrils, called barbels. They use these to touch and taste the seabed.

Sharks have a super-sensitive sense of smell. They can sniff out one part of blood in one million parts of water.

Fact!

Some sharks may be able to track their prey by smell from up to a mile (1.6 km) away.

45

Sensing Movement

Animals that live underwater can tell when another creature is approaching because the water around them moves, or vibrates.

Sharks have developed a special sense organ to detect these vibrations from far away. Tiny, sensitive pores called **ampullae of Lorenzini** around their snout help them identify living things, too.

Feeling movement

Sharks' special sense organ, the lateral line system, runs down each side of the body and around the head. It is lined with hairs that detect the vibrations caused by water currents, and by other animals moving in the water.

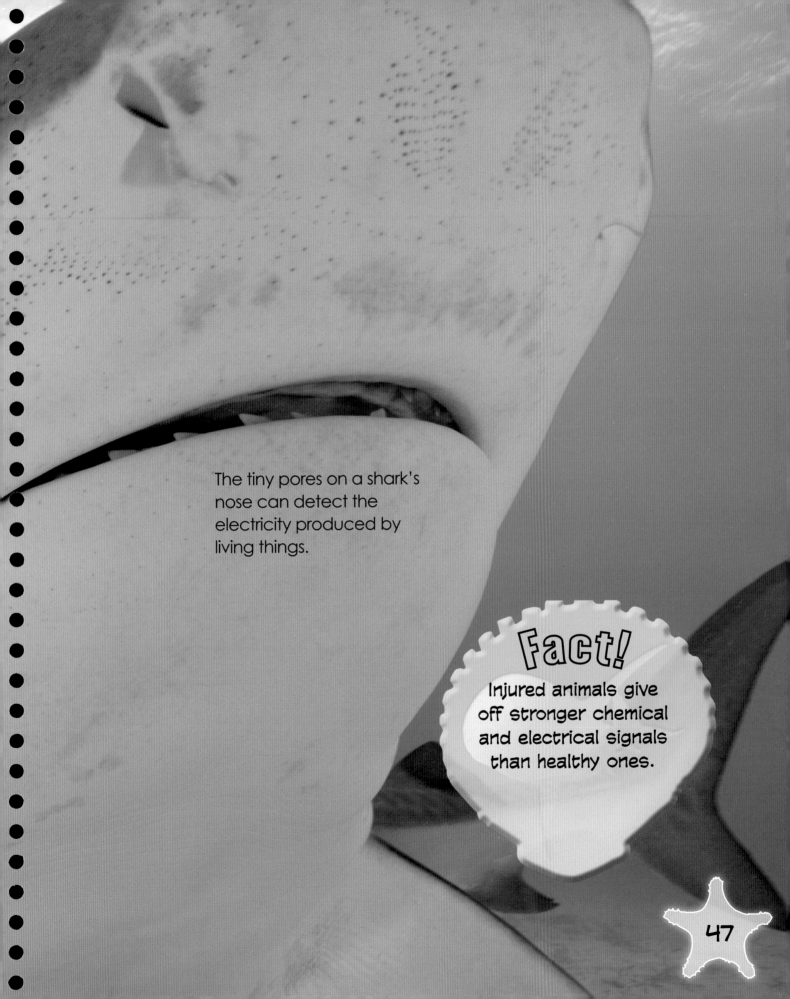

The tiny pores on a shark's nose can detect the electricity produced by living things.

Fact!
Injured animals give off stronger chemical and electrical signals than healthy ones.

Smart Sharks

Sharks act mostly by instinct, which means they behave in a way that comes naturally to them. Scientists have recently discovered that sharks also have the ability to learn.

Learning to behave

Sharks can learn from experience and change their behavior. Some sharks learn to follow fishing boats, so they can scavenge any dead fish thrown overboard. They have even been taught to travel through a maze to reach food in an aquarium.

In captivity, sharks learn when it is feeding time.

At some tourist sites, sharks have learned that food will be put out for them every day. When they arrive to feed, divers are ready to photograph them.

Fact!
Sharks may nudge and butt divers, because they have learned that divers sometimes give them food.

Friend or Foe?

Parasites are animals that live on, or in, the body of another animal—the host—usually causing it harm. Many sharks have parasites, such as lice or worms, which can cause them pain or make them sick, although some visitors are more welcome.

Cleaner fish

Wrasse are small fish that live in and around coral reefs. They are known as cleaner wrasse, because they like to nibble bits of dead skin or parasites from the bodies of other animals. Some sharks visit the coral reefs where wrasse collect to encourage the wrasse to nibble at their parasites.

This cleaner wrasse is feeding from the mouth of a goatfish.

Fact!

Cookie cutter sharks bite into the bodies of other sharks, grabbing a chunk of flesh with their teeth.

Remoras, or shark suckers, grab onto sharks with their sucking mouth to hitch a ride.

Hammerhead Shark

Hammerhead sharks are the strangest looking of all sharks. Their head is wide and flat, and their eyes are situated at the very ends, or lobes. This odd shape helps them to change direction, and gives them wider vision.

Spiky dinner

Hammerheads like to eat rays, such as electric rays, eagle rays, and especially stingrays. They do not seem to mind being stung by the venomous stingrays.

Distinctive head shape

First dorsal fin

Fact File

Gill slits

Pelvic fin

LENGTH   Up to 16 feet (5 meters)

HABITAT   Shallow water, near coasts

DEPTH   Usually close to the surface, around 66 feet (20 meters)

RANGE   Warm waters around the world

Hammerheads swish their heads from side to side to get an all-round view.

Close Cousins

Most fish have a bony skeleton, but sharks belong to a group of fish that have a skeleton made of cartilage instead of bone.

Cartilage, which also supports our noses and ears, is bendier than bone. Fish with skeletons made of cartilage include skates and rays as well as sharks.

The common skate is the world's largest skate, growing up to 8 ft (2.5 m).

Skates lie in wait for their prey, or bury themselves under sand and gravel, so they are completely hidden from view.

Colorful skates

Skates live in oceans around the world, in shallow water and close to the shore. They have a wide, flat body and are often highly colored and patterned, so they are well camouflaged on the seabed, where they stay most of the time.

Fact!

Skates swim by gently rolling their enormous pectoral fins, to glide gracefully through the water.

Stinging Cousins

With their large, flat body, rays look similar to skates. However, unlike skates, they give birth to live young.

Rays are usually larger than skates, and are kite-shaped. They have whip-like tails with one or two stinging spines, which they use to defend themselves if attacked.

The manta ray can grow to an incredible 26 ft (8 m) in width. Thankfully, mantas are harmless to humans.

Electric rays use electricity, which their body makes, to attack their prey. A single flash of electricity can stun, or even kill, another fish—and can give a human a nasty shock.

Stingrays

Stingrays have venomous spines near the base of their tail. They often rest on the seabed. If they are disturbed, stingrays lash out with their tail. The stings are painful to humans, but rarely deadly.

The stingray lives in the coral reefs of tropical seas.

Fact!

Only four mantas are kept in aquariums around the world. Their massive size makes them hard to keep!

Shark Attack

Many people are scared of being attacked by sharks when they are in the ocean, but most sharks are harmless. Only about 40 species have been known to attack humans.

The world's three most dangerous sharks are the great white, tiger, and bull sharks. In parts of the world where shark attacks have happened, such as Australia and South Africa, many beaches are protected by shark nets.

Fact!

Worldwide, there have been only about 200 unprovoked shark attacks on divers in the last 100 years.

Shark attacks

Occasionally sharks attack humans because they mistake them for other animals. If an injured person in the water was bleeding, for example, a shark would be attracted by the scent of the blood.

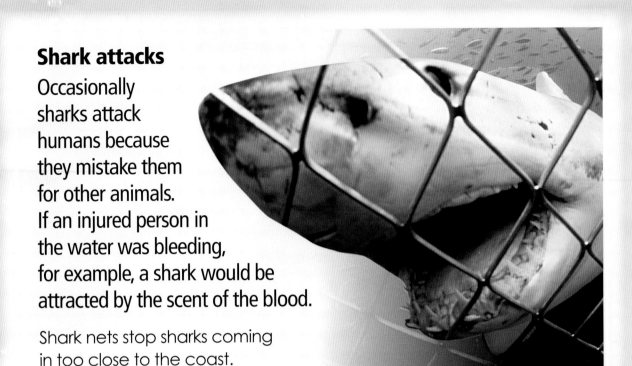

Shark nets stop sharks coming in too close to the coast.

Many people fear great white sharks but tiger sharks are more dangerous.

Discovering Sharks

Scientists observe sharks by diving with them, sometimes in the safety of cages. They also find out about sharks' behavior by tagging.

Tagging involves attaching a clip to a shark's fin, which sends signals back to a base. The signals enable scientists to follow the shark's journeys, finding out how far it travels and where it goes.

A diver can watch and film a great white shark from the safety of a cage.

Fact!

A blue shark tagged near New York was caught 16 months later, 3,600 miles (6,000 km) away, off the coast of Brazil.

60

Tourist thrill

Tourists enjoy the thrill of getting close to sharks. Shark tourism helps people to learn about sharks, and it makes money for local businesses. Feeding sharks is popular, although it makes sharks less fearful of humans—and could lead to more shark attacks.

This diver wears a metal suit for protection while he feeds a reef shark.

A scientist attaches a numbered tag to a shark's fin.

Sharks Under Threat

Scientists estimate that nearly half of all shark species are at some risk of becoming **extinct**, which means they could disappear from our oceans forever.

Up to 120 million sharks are caught and killed by people every year. About one-quarter of all shark species are killed for food—millions of sharks are caught every year just to make shark-fin soup, a delicacy in Asia.

Fact!

Shark populations are now only one-tenth of what they used to be. Humans are responsible for killing the rest.

Fishing boats have equipment that helps them to find, and catch, sharks in the deep ocean.

MAUi III
1054

RITA VICTO
4694

BUITRI

The future

Our oceans need sharks. They are part of the complex system of living things that all rely on one another to survive. We can all help by not buying shark products, and by learning more about these beautiful fish.

Whales

Intelligent and gentle—whales are unique animals. These mighty mammals breathe air, but they swim underwater. Whales can travel to the very depths of the oceans, where few humans have ever ventured.

The Whale

The blue whale is the largest animal that has ever existed. It is just one of many types of whale that swim in the world's oceans.

Whales are close relatives of dolphins and porpoises and, like them, have flippers, a long body, and no back limbs. The biggest whales live for around 100 years.

Whales often leap out of the water. This is called **breaching**.

66

Whales are not fish

Whales are **mammals**. Mammal is the name given to any animal that produces milk for its young. All mammals have at least some hairs on their body. Whales are almost hairless, with just a few bristles in their nostrils.

A blue whale gliding through the water.

Fact!

The blue whale grows up to 100 ft (30 m) long and weighs about 150 tons (165 tonnes)—that's as much as 30 African elephants.

Whale Types

There are about 50 different species, or types, of whales, which are divided into two groups.

One group is the baleen whales, which includes humpback whales, gray whales, and fin whales. Baleen whales have huge plates instead of teeth, which strain food from the water.

Toothed whales

The other group is called the toothed whales. This group includes most whales, such as sperm whales, pilot whales, and narwhals. They are smaller than the baleen whales. Toothed whales hunt fish, squid, seals, and sometimes other animals.

Toothed whales, such as this beluga, have small teeth that they use to grip fish and other prey.

The humpback whale swallows a huge mouthful of water and fish as it comes to the surface.

69

Where Do Whales Live?

Whales are found in all the oceans of the world, including the coldest ones such as the Southern and Arctic Oceans.

Some whales live in very deep water, where it is pitch black. Many swim long distances each year, from cold waters to warmer places and back again.

Fact!

Narwhals live farther north than any other whale in the Arctic. They form groups of several thousand.

Whales are found in all the oceans of the world, but they are more common in colder waters.

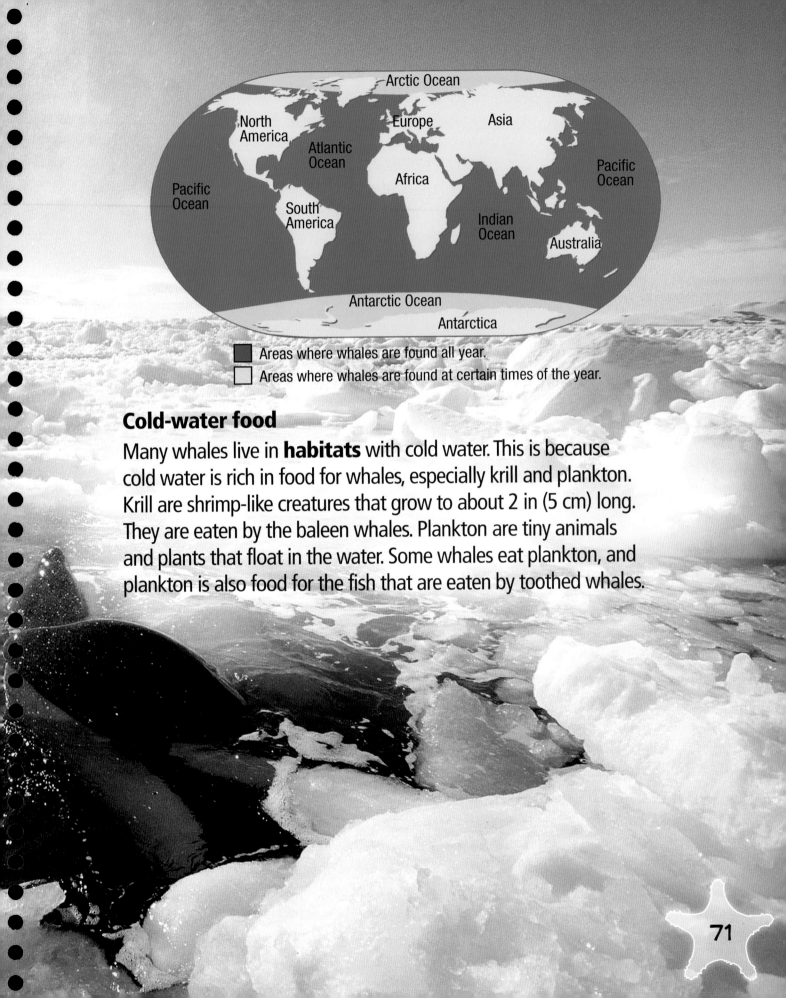

Arctic Ocean

North America

Europe

Asia

Atlantic Ocean

Pacific Ocean

Pacific Ocean

Africa

South America

Indian Ocean

Australia

Antarctic Ocean

Antarctica

Areas where whales are found all year.
Areas where whales are found at certain times of the year.

Cold-water food

Many whales live in **habitats** with cold water. This is because cold water is rich in food for whales, especially krill and plankton. Krill are shrimp-like creatures that grow to about 2 in (5 cm) long. They are eaten by the baleen whales. Plankton are tiny animals and plants that float in the water. Some whales eat plankton, and plankton is also food for the fish that are eaten by toothed whales.

Giving Birth

Female whales may be pregnant for between nine and seventeen months, depending on the species.

Many female whales swim to a special place where they give birth to a single **calf**. As soon as her calf is born, the mother pushes it to the surface for its first breath of air.

Calves of the larger whales, like this humpback, are about 13 ft (4 m) long at birth.

The calf stays close
to its mother's side.

Whale calves

The female whale feeds her calf on milk that
is rich in fat, so it grows quickly. The calf has
to learn how to breathe without swallowing
water and how to stay upright in the water.
The calf practises swimming and, after six
weeks, can do a complete roll underwater.

Fact!

Female California
gray whales are known
as devilfish because they
are very aggressive
toward any animal
that comes near
their calves.

Young whales are very playful.

Growing Up

Whale calves drink their mother's milk for up to a year. Then they start to eat adult food.

Calves are very playful and love to jump out of the water and smash down with a loud splash. They roll in the water and slap the surface with their fins.

A short-fin pilot whale and calf travel close together through the ocean.

Staying close

Calves follow their mother. By staying close, they learn where to find food and which routes to take on long journeys. Some young whales leave their mother once they are **weaned,** but others stay close by for a long time. Sperm whales stay with their mother for ten years. Some whales live with their mother as part of a family group, or **pod**.

Fact!

Young baleen whales have been seen to breach (jump out of the water) more than 80 times an hour while playing.

Sperm Whale

Sperm whales are the largest carnivores—meat-eaters—on the planet. These mighty hunters pursue their prey downward, through the dark and murky ocean waters. They gobble up massive quantities of squid, fish, and octopuses.

Diving deep

A sperm whale can dive down up to a mile (1.6 kilometers) to reach its favorite food, squid and octopuses. It can stay under the water for up to two hours.

The sperm whale's large tail fin, called a fluke, helps it to move through the water at great speed.

Sperm whales are often spotted in pods, or groups, of around 15 or 20 animals.

Fact File

Fluke

Rough, creased skin

Square head

LENGTH 36–65 feet (11–20 meters)
HABITAT Deep ocean waters
DEPTH Dives to depths of up to one mile (1.6 km)
RANGE Worldwide

Underwater Living

When whales come to the surface, they breathe out so hard that a jet of air and water bursts out of their blowhole.

Unlike fish and many other underwater animals, whales cannot breathe in water. They must swim to the surface to breathe air.

Whales do not breathe through their mouth, but through a large nostril called a **blowhole** on the top of their head. Just before a whale dives under the water, a flap covers the blowhole. Whales can stay underwater for a long time before they have to surface again.

Keeping warm

Whales have to keep warm in cold water. They have a thick layer of fat, called **blubber**, under their skin. The fat traps heat in the whale's body so it stays warm.

Sperm whales have a huge, square head, which is filled with a waxy substance called spermaceti. This may help them dive.

Senses

Whales have well-developed senses that help them find out about their surroundings.

Whales' hearing is very sensitive, but they do not have ears on the outside of their head. Instead, there are two tiny openings on the side of the head, which lead to internal ears. Whales have small eyes and cannot see very well. However, this is not a problem, because they often swim in dark water.

The tiny eyes of this blue whale are behind its mouth. Whales are used to living in murky water, where they can see objects only up to about 3 ft (1 m) away.

Echolocation

Toothed whales detect objects using a method called **echolocation**. The whale sends out high-pitched clicks, which bounce off objects and return to the whale as echoes. By listening to the echoes, the whale can figure out the shape and position of objects, including its prey.

81

Communication

No one is sure why male humpback whales sing. It might be to attract a female, or to tell other males that they are in the area.

Whales communicate in many ways. They make different sounds, such as whistles, trills, moans, and squeals.

Whales can hear the sounds of other whales from far away. Breaching and lobtailing (slapping their tails on the surface) are other ways whales communicate with one another.

Humpback songs

Male humpback whales' songs contain up to 30 different sounds and can last for 30 minutes. When the whale gets to the end of his song, he starts from the beginning again. He can keep this up for hours! At certain depths, the whales' songs travel for thousands of miles through the water.

Fact!

The moans of the blue whale are the loudest sound made by any animal and much louder than even a jet engine.

This whale is lobtailing. It is sticking its tail out of the water and will slap it on the surface to make a loud sound.

Whale Journeys

Many whales make long journeys each year. They spend part of the year in cold waters and then swim to warmer waters. This annual trip is called migration.

Each year, whales spend several months in warm waters, where they often give birth to their calves. Young calves do not have a thick layer of blubber, so they could not survive in cold water. Then they swim to their cold water feeding areas. The whales swim together in groups and follow the same routes each year. Calves swim with their mothers to learn the route.

This blue whale and her calf are migrating along the coast of California to their feeding grounds in the Arctic.

Whales stick their head out of the water to check for landmarks and to see if there are any other whales around—this is called spyhopping.

Bowhead Whale

Bowhead whales live in freezing waters, and their body is lined with blubber, two feet (60 centimeters) thick, to keep them warm. These massive mammals have an enormous appetite—they need to eat about two tons (1,800 kilos) of food every day just to survive.

Bowhead whales can even swim under floating ice, using their massive head to break through.

Baleen plates

Instead of teeth, bowhead whales have horny fringes called baleen plates. These act like a giant sieve. The whales use them to strain and collect plankton and krill—the tiny creatures that are their main source of food.

Baleen plates are made from keratin, the same substance as your hair and nails!

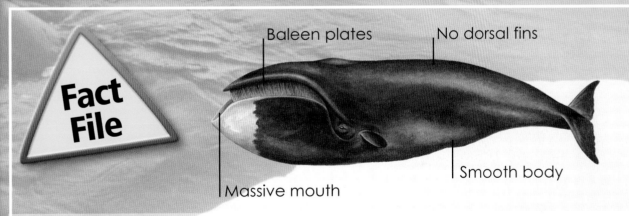

Fact File

Baleen plates

No dorsal fins

Massive mouth

Smooth body

LENGTH	45–59 feet (14–18 meters)
HABITAT	Cold oceans and seas
DEPTH	Mostly stays in shallow water
RANGE	Arctic and sub-Arctic waters

Whales Under Threat

Whales around the world are under threat. For a long time, whales were hunted for their oil and meat. So many whales were killed that many species almost became extinct.

Although many countries decided that whales should no longer be hunted, some disagreed, and these have carried on killing whales. Also, whales need plenty of food, and sometimes people take too much fish and krill from the oceans and do not leave enough for whales and other sea animals.

These people are watching gray whales off the coast of California.

Fact!

The California gray whale has been taken off the list of **endangered** animals because its numbers have increased to normal levels.

Whale conservation

It is important that whales are protected so that they do not die out completely. Whale watching is enjoyed by many people and brings money into coastal towns, so local people have a good reason to save the whales.

In the past, huge numbers of sperm whales were killed for their oil.

Dolphins and Porpoises

Dolphins and porpoises are elegant, graceful swimmers of the world's oceans. They often play in shallow coastal waters, where people can watch them, and they sometimes follow fishing boats. Playful and friendly, dolphins are also the most intelligent animals in the oceans.

Dolphins and Porpoises

Like whales, dolphins and porpoises have a pair of lungs rather than gills. This means that, unlike fish, they have to come to the surface of the water to breathe.

Dolphins and porpoises are sociable animals, and they live in family groups, called pods. The female is called a sow, the male a bull, and the young are called calves.

Even large dolphins like to leap out of the water when they swim close to the surface.

Marine mammals

Dolphins and porpoises are mammals. This means that the females give birth to live young and feed them milk. Unlike most other mammals, dolphins and porpoises do not have body hair. Their skin is sleek, smooth, and rubbery to the touch. The largest dolphins are orcas, which grow up to 30 feet (9 meters) in length. Some of the smallest, Hector's dolphins, are about 4 feet (1.2 meters) long.

Dolphins are mammals and have flippers instead of legs.

Dolphin pods sometimes join together to form a super-pod of several thousand animals.

Dolphin and Porpoise Types

There are 37 types, or species, of dolphin and six types of porpoise. Most porpoises stay in the sea, whereas five species of dolphin live in rivers.

The small spinner dolphin lives mainly in tropical waters.

Dolphin or porpoise?

Dolphins usually have a long, slender snout, called a beak, whereas porpoises have a rounded head. Also, dolphins have curved dorsal fins and porpoises have triangular ones.

River dolphins

River dolphins are small—some are just 3 feet (1 meter) long. River dolphins have a long, slender beak and a large, bulging forehead. Their eyes are small and, unlike other dolphins, they have a neck.

Most of the long-beaked river dolphins, like these ones, have poor eyesight.

Where Do Dolphins and Porpoises Live?

Dolphins and porpoises live in all the oceans and seas, even in the very cold waters of the Arctic, and in some of the world's major rivers.

Some, such as the common dolphin and bottlenose dolphin, can be found all around the world. Others, such as the Pacific white-sided dolphin, live only in certain oceans. Some types of dolphins and porpoises prefer to stay close to land in shallow water, but others like to live in deeper waters far out in the ocean.

The Amazon River dolphin lives in the Amazon and Orinoco rivers of South America.

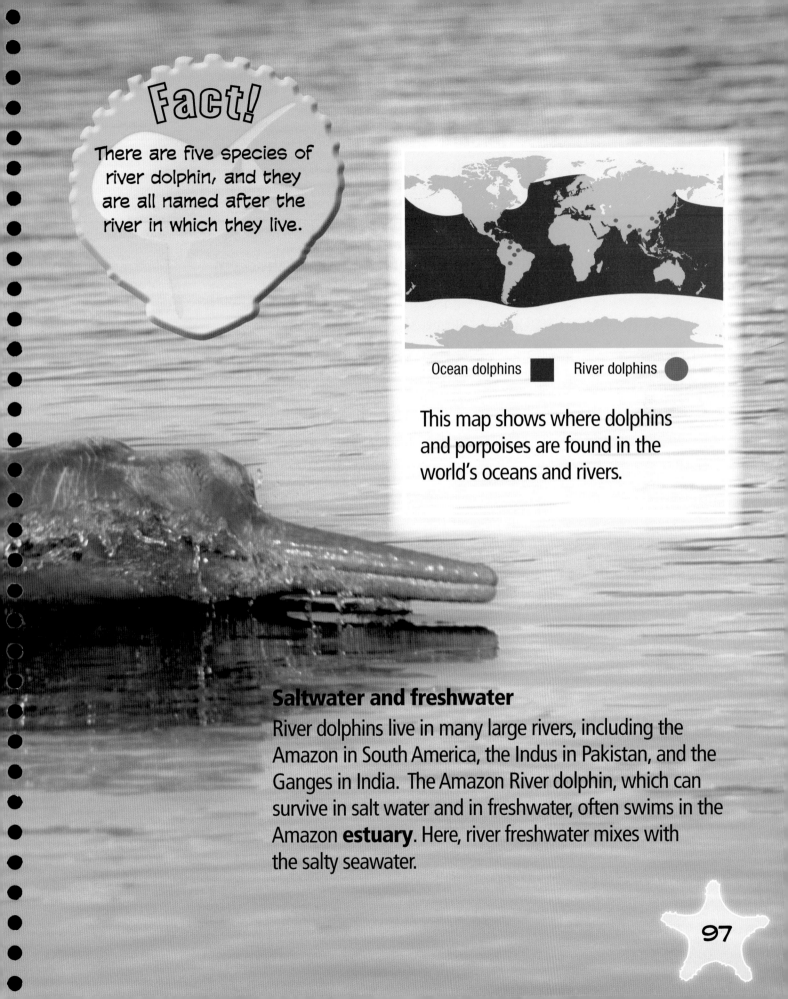

Fact!

There are five species of river dolphin, and they are all named after the river in which they live.

This map shows where dolphins and porpoises are found in the world's oceans and rivers.

Ocean dolphins ■   River dolphins ●

Saltwater and freshwater

River dolphins live in many large rivers, including the Amazon in South America, the Indus in Pakistan, and the Ganges in India. The Amazon River dolphin, which can survive in salt water and in freshwater, often swims in the Amazon **estuary**. Here, river freshwater mixes with the salty seawater.

Giving Birth

After a bull and sow dolphin have come together to mate, the sow will be pregnant for one year.

A sow then gives birth to one calf in the water, which is born tail first. Soon after the birth, the sow pushes her calf to the water's surface so that it can take its first breath. As dolphins breathe through a blowhole on the top of their head, the newborn calf has to learn when to open and close its blowhole to avoid breathing in water!

A newborn bottlenose dolphin calf weighs about 13–18 lbs (6–8 kilos) and is up to 3 ft (1 m) long.

First month

The hungry calf quickly starts feeding on its mother's milk, which is rich in fat and helps the calf to grow quickly. During the first month, the calf stays close to its mother's side. Her movements in the water help to pull the calf gently along.

Growing Up

The young calf feeds on its mother's milk for about one year after it is born. When it is three months old, however, the calf's first teeth appear and it starts to eat fish as well.

Dolphins enjoy racing through the water alongside boats.

Fact!

Mother dolphins may teach their young to put bits of sponge on their beak for protection while hunting for food on the rough seabed.

Learning from play

Dolphin calves spend a lot of time playing with their mother and with other calves in the pod. They dart about the waves created by boats and leap out of the surf. Playing is important for young dolphins, as it teaches them how to communicate with each other and how to hunt for food.

By playing together, young dolphins learn many skills that they will need as adults.

Living in Pods

Most pods contain about ten dolphins or porpoises, although the biggest pods can have many thousands of animals in them.

A typical pod is made up of sows and their calves together with a few bulls. Sometimes, dolphins or porpoises that are not related will form a pod.

Leaving the pod

A calf is cared for by its mother for the first two years of its life, sometimes even longer. After this, a female calf usually stays in her mother's pod, whereas a male calf joins another pod.

Hunting together

When out hunting, members of the pod communicate by whistling. Sometimes, pods join together to form large hunting herds. If a mother joins a hunting group, her calves are often looked after by other sows in the pod.

The tiger shark is a predator of dolphins and porpoises.

Fact!

When under attack, members of a pod work together to chase off the predator—usually an orca or a shark.

This pod of spinner dolphins is made up of sows, calves, and a few bulls.

Orca

Orcas, also known as killer whales, are the largest and most aggressive of all dolphins. They live in all the world's oceans, from freezing Antarctic waters to tropical seas.

Clever killers

Orcas are famous for their great skill at chasing and catching prey. They will sometimes leap onto ice floes to catch seals, or even tip slabs of ice over, so penguins, or other prey, fall into the water.

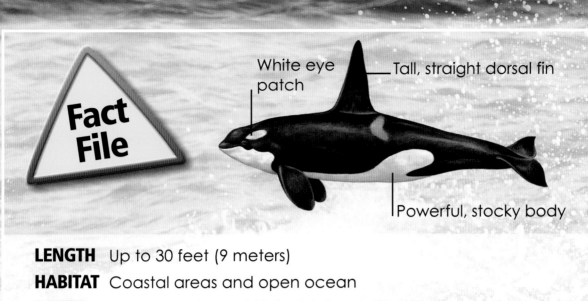

Fact File

White eye patch

Tall, straight dorsal fin

Powerful, stocky body

LENGTH	Up to 30 feet (9 meters)
HABITAT	Coastal areas and open ocean
DEPTH	Shallow water to 200 feet (about 60 meters)
RANGE	Worldwide except extreme north and south

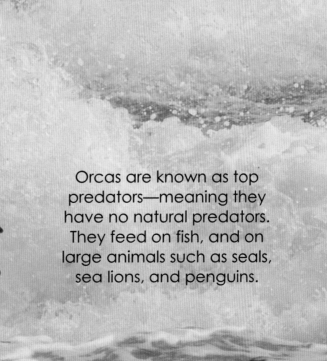

Orcas are known as top predators—meaning they have no natural predators. They feed on fish, and on large animals such as seals, sea lions, and penguins.

A Life in Water

Dolphins and porpoises spend their whole life in water, rising to the surface to breathe.

When they surface, they open the blowhole on the top of their head and let out the air in their lungs with a spurt. This blows away water in their blowhole so that when they breathe in again, water does not get into their lungs.

Fact!

The deepest dive recorded for a bottlenose dolphin is an incredible 1,000 ft (about 300 m).

Keeping warm

Dolphins and porpoises need to keep their body heat at 96°F (36°C)—almost the same temperature as a human being. To stay warm dolphins and porpoises have a thick layer of fat under their skin called blubber. The blubber traps heat in their body and keeps them warm in the cold ocean waters.

A dolphin's blowhole is on the top of its head, behind its bulging forehead.

Dolphins come to the surface to breathe every two minutes or so. But they can hold their breath for longer when they need to.

Senses

Dolphins and porpoises use their senses to find their way around and catch their prey.

They do not have a sense of smell, but their ears, which are inside their skull, give them excellent hearing. Most dolphins and porpoises, apart from the river dolphins, also have good eyesight. The Ganges River dolphin is completely blind.

When dolphins are under the water, special greasy tears protect their eyes from the stinging salt in seawater.

Like whales, dolphins and porpoises can find their way, and locate prey, using sound. This is called echolocation.

Whistles and clicks

The dolphin uses its **melon** to transmit lots of whistles and clicks. These sounds pass through the water and bounce off things to make the echoes that the dolphin uses for echolocation. By listening to these echoes, a dolphin can work out exactly where things are.

The melon is located in the bulging forehead of dolphins and porpoises.

Hunting

Dolphins and porpoises are carnivores, or meat eaters. They eat mainly fish, such as anchovies, mackerel, herring, and cod, as well as squid.

Dolphins and porpoises use echolocation to find their fish prey. When the members of a pod find a **shoal** of fish, they surround it so that the shoal cannot escape. Then one or two members of the pod start to swim through the middle to catch the fish.

This dolphin is splitting a school of fish by swimming through the middle.

Fact!

The blind Ganges River dolphin drags a flipper along the seabed to find small prey in the mud.

Swallowed whole

Dolphins and porpoises have small, sharp teeth, which they use to grip a fish's slippery body. As they cannot chew, dolphins and porpoises swallow small fish whole. Before swallowing, however, they carefully position the fish headfirst to prevent the spines along the back of the fish from sticking in their throat. If a fish is too large to swallow whole, dolphins will rip it up with their cone-shaped teeth before swallowing it in pieces.

Dolphins trap small fish between their teeth and then swallow them whole.

Communication

Dolphins and porpoises make many sounds to communicate, including squeaks, grunts, trills, and even moans.

These sounds travel quickly through water, sometimes over long distances. Scientists believe each dolphin has its own type of whistle sound, and that many dolphins can recognize each other by the sound they make.

Fact!

When a calf is born, it learns to recognize its mother's whistle, so that it will always be able to find her—even in a large pod.

Dolphins are very talkative and call to each other all the time.

Dolphins make a lot of noise when they crash down onto the water's surface.

Slapping the water

Dolphins and porpoises also communicate by touching and butting each other, or by leaping out of the water. They also slap the surface of the water with their tails to make a noise that other dolphins or porpoises will hear.

Spinner Dolphin

Spinner dolphins are athletic and sociable animals. They are spectacular acrobats and they like to swim with other animals, including humpback whales and yellow tuna fish.

Spinning through the air

The spinner dolphin can leap out of the water and spin three times in the air! Some scientists think they do this not for fun but to try and shake off the parasitic remoras or suckerfish that stick to their skin.

Spinner dolphins travel in huge groups, or herds, that number several thousand.

Fact File

Triangular dorsal fin

Slender, muscular body

Long snout

Pointed flipper

LENGTH 4–6 ½ feet (1.3 to 2 meters)
HABITAT Tropical waters, coasts, coral reefs
DEPTH Shallow swimmers
RANGE In warm waters worldwide

Dolphins Under Threat

Dolphins and porpoises, especially river dolphins, are under threat all around the world. Each year, thousands are killed by hunters or die in fishing nets.

Some dolphins even die from lack of food because people have taken too many fish from the waters where they feed. Pollution from chemicals and sewage also harms many dolphins and porpoises.

Dolphin-watching trips are popular with tourists in many parts of the world.

Fact!

The rarest porpoise is the vaquita, of which there are only 200 still alive. These are found in the Gulf of California.

This rare vaquita porpoise was caught up in a fisherman's net and drowned.

Helping dolphins and porpoises

There are many organizations, such as the Whale and Dolphin Conservation Society, that are working to safeguard dolphins and porpoises. More and more marine nature reserves now exist where dolphins and porpoises are protected from hunting and fishing. Many fishermen are now helping too, by using special nets and fishing lines that do not trap dolphins and porpoises.

Glossary

ampullae of Lorenzini tiny sensors near the front of a shark's head. These detect electrical signals produced when an animal moves.

blowhole the hole in the top of the head of a dolphin, porpoise, or whale that is used for breathing

blubber a thick layer of fat under the skin

breaching when a whale jumps above the surface of the water

calf a baby or young whale

camouflage an animal's coloring that blends in with its background

cetacean a group of marine mammals that includes whales, dolphins, and porpoises

echolocation a way of finding where things are by sending out sounds and listening for echoes that come back

endangered in danger of dying out

estuary the mouth of a river

extinct no longer any left alive

filter feeder an animal that sieves, or removes, food such as small plants and animals from the water to eat

gills organs inside the body of a fish used for breathing in water

gill slits slits, or gaps, in the body wall where water passes out of the body

habitat the place in which an animal or plant lives

invertebrate an animal without a backbone

mammal an animal that gives birth to live young, rather than laying eggs. Female mammals produce milk to feed their young.

melon a structure in the forehead of a dolphin or porpoise used for echolocation

migration a journey made each year to find food or to breed

parasite an animal that depends on another animal and causes it harm

pectoral fins fins that are positioned just behind the gill slits

plankton tiny plants and animals that float in the upper layers of the ocean

pod a family group of whales

predator an animal that hunts other animals for food

pregnant a female animal that has a baby, or babies, developing inside her

prey an animal that is hunted and eaten by other animals

shoal a group of fish

sonar a device used by submarines and ships to find objects in water and calculate how far away they are

species a group of individuals which have the same appearance and are able to breed and produce young together

weaned changed from milk to an adult diet

Index